Overview *Hello, I'm Joe*

Hannah is teaching her parakeet to speak, and one day he flies away.

Reading Vocabulary Words

frightened
parakeet
balcony

High-Frequency Words

bump	help
clean	exercise
called	would
gray	breakfast

Building Future Vocabulary

* These vocabulary words do not appear in this text. They are provided to develop related oral vocabulary that first appears in future texts.

Words:	clutch	recognize	sob
Levels:	Gold	Silver	Gold

Comprehension Strategy
Recognizing cause and effect

Fluency Skill
Varying the use of loudness and softness when reading phrases

Phonics Skill
Identifying and reading contractions (I'm, you'd, didn't, don't, won't, mustn't, you've)

Reading-Writing Connection
Writing an ad

Home Connection
Send home one of the Flying Colors Take-Home books for children to share with their families.

Differentiated Instruction
Before reading the text, query children to discover their level of understanding of the comprehension strategy — Recognizing cause and effect. As you work together, provide additional support to children who show a beginning mastery of the strategy.

Focus on ELL
- Talk with children about birds, and help them identify the different parts of a bird. Help children use the correct English terms.

- Have children discuss what they would need in order to take care of a pet bird.

Using This Teaching Version

1 Before Reading

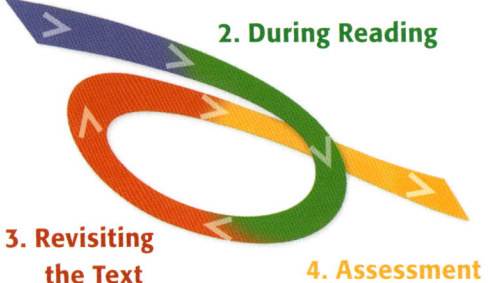

1. Before Reading

2. During Reading

3. Revisiting the Text

4. Assessment

This Teaching Version will assist you in directing children through the process of reading.

1. Begin with Before Reading to familiarize children with the book's content. Select the skills and strategies that meet the needs of your children.

2. Next, go to During Reading to help children become familiar with the text, and then to read individually on their own.

3. Then, go back to Revisiting the Text and select those specific activities that meet children's needs.

4. Finally, finish with Assessment to confirm children are ready to move forward to the next text.

Building Background

- Write the word *frightened* on the board. Read it aloud. Ask *What kinds of things can frighten a person?* (the dark, loud noises, snakes) *What kinds of things frighten a bird?* (cats, noises)

- Introduce the book by reading the title, talking about the cover illustration, and sharing the overview.

Building Future Vocabulary
Use Interactive Modeling Card: Meaning Map

- Discuss the word *clutch*. Ask children for a sentence using the word *clutch*. (She *clutch*ed the paper in her hand.)

- With children complete the Meaning Map for the word *clutch*.

Introduction to Reading Vocabulary

- On blank cards write: *frightened*, *parakeet*, and *balcony*. Read them aloud. Tell children these words will appear in the text of *Hello, I'm Joe*.

- Use each word in a sentence for understanding.

Introduction to Comprehension Strategy

- Explain that *cause and effect* means that one action makes something else happen. Have children look at the title page. Ask *Do you suppose the birdcage is empty because someone left the door open?*

- Ask *What is the first action, or cause?* (Someone opened the cage door.) *What is the result, or effect?* (The bird flew out of the cage.)

- Tell children they will be looking for actions that cause results, or cause and effect, in *Hello, I'm Joe.*

Introduction to Phonics

- Explain how to shorten two words into contractions using an apostrophe.

- Write the words **did not** and **must not** on the board. Show how to form the contractions **didn't** and **mustn't**.

- Make a list of common contractions on chart paper.

- Have children look for other contractions as they read *Hello, I'm Joe.*

Modeling Fluency

- Read aloud a few sentences from page 2, showing how to vary loudness and softness.

- Talk about how we can use our voice to increase the drama or excitement of a story.

2 During Reading

Book Talk

Beginning on page T4, use the During Reading notes on the left-hand side to engage children in a book talk. On page 16, follow with Individual Reading.

During Reading

Book Talk

- **Phonics Skill** Ask a volunteer to read the title aloud. Have children point to the contraction *I'm.* Explain that *I'm* is a contraction of *I* and *am.*

- Have children look at the title page and read the chapter titles. Ask *Who do you suppose moves "like a golden arrow"?* (the yellow bird in the story) Explain that the bird is a parakeet. Ask children if they know anyone with a parakeet or have seen one in a store.

➡ *Turn to page 2 — Book Talk*

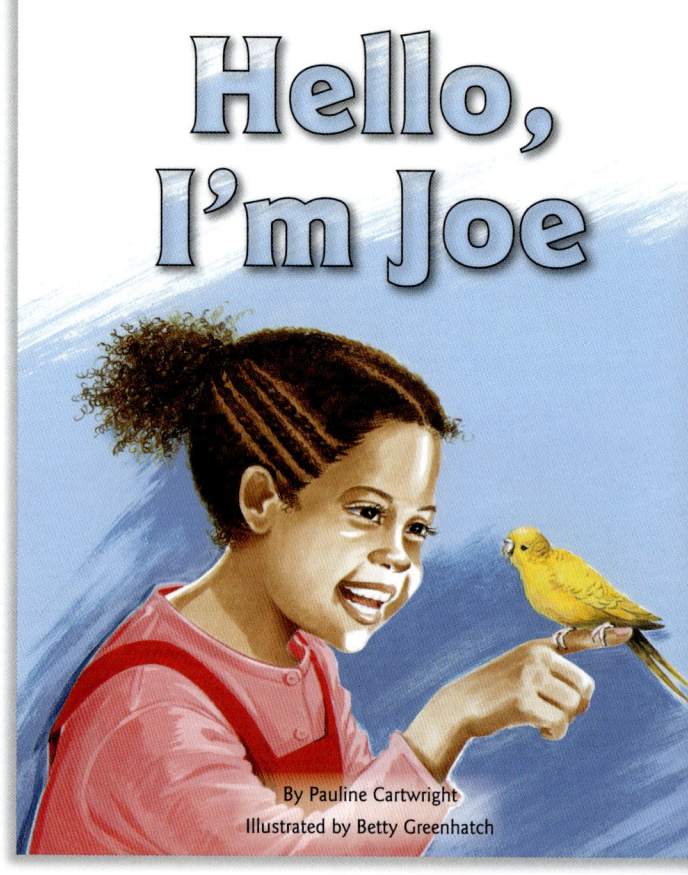

T4

Revisiting the Text

Hello, I'm Joe

By Pauline Cartwright
Illustrated by Betty Greenhatch

Chapter 1	**Like a Golden Arrow**	2
Chapter 2	**A Bump Under the Jacket**	8
Chapter 3	**At Last!**	12

Future Vocabulary
- Look at the cover illustration. Ask *What is Hannah doing?* (trying to teach Joe to say his name) *Do you think Joe recognizes his name?*

Now revisit pages 2–3

During Reading

Book Talk

- Ask *What is the girl holding on her finger?* (a parakeet) *Where does the parakeet probably live?* (in the cage) Have children locate the words *parakeet* on page 2 and *balcony* on page 3.

- **Comprehension Strategy** Say *The girl is smiling at the parakeet. Why?* (because she likes the parakeet) Explain this cause and effect: Hannah smiles at Joe because she likes him.

- **Phonics Skill** Have children find the word *you'd* on page 2. Show on the board how *you'd* is formed from the words *you* and *would*.

Turn to page 4 — Book Talk

Chapter 1
Like a Golden Arrow

For a pet, Hannah had a yellow parakeet she called Joe. She tried to teach him to talk.

"Hello, I'm Joe," she said, over and over again. Joe never said it back.

"I do wish you'd try," Hannah would say.

Revisiting the Text

Joe was a good pet to have in an apartment because he didn't need a field or a yard to live in. His home was a cage that hung on a hook in the corner of the living room. Hannah's dad had put a hook on the balcony, too, so that Joe's cage could sometimes be hung outside.

Hannah had to clean the cage and make sure there was always food and water inside. Now and again, she gave Joe some exercise by letting him fly around the living room. After a while, Hannah would let him land on her finger and would put him back in his cage.

Future Vocabulary
- Ask *How is Joe able to stay on Hannah's finger?* (He is clutching her finger.) Explain that *clutch* means "to grasp tightly."
- Have children write a sentence using the word *clutch*.

Now revisit pages 4–5

3

During Reading

Book Talk

- Have children study the illustration on page 4. Ask *Where do you think Hannah lives?* (in a big city) *What clues tell you this?* (skyscrapers, small balcony)

- Have children find the word *balcony* in the text. Ask children what a balcony is and where they might find one.

- **Comprehension Strategy** Ask *What is happening in these illustrations?* (The bird is flying away.) Ask *What happened before the parakeet escaped?* (Someone opened the door.) *Which is the cause and which is the effect?* (Cause: someone opened the door; effect: the parakeet flew away.)

Turn to page 6 — Book Talk

One day Hannah's dad was working on the balcony.

Hannah called to him, "Dad, don't open the door because Joe is exercising inside."

When Dad had finished his work, he forgot what Hannah had said. He opened the door, and Joe flew straight out! Hannah saw him going, like a little golden arrow, off over the rooftops.

Revisiting the Text

"Joe's gone!" cried Hannah, and she burst into tears.

Dad held her close while she cried. "Oh, Hannah!" he said. "I'm so sorry."

Future Vocabulary

- Ask children for examples of things they recognize. (people, words, animals) Say *What kinds of sounds can you recognize?* (voices, music, noises)

- Ask *What items do you recognize on the balcony?* (plants, bushes) Ask *Do you recognize the tool Dad is holding in his hand?* (a pair of clippers)

Now revisit pages 6–7

During Reading

Book Talk

- Have children locate the words *frightened* and *balcony* on page 6.

- **Fluency Skill** Have children read page 6 aloud, varying their use of loud and soft voices to create drama.

- **Comprehension Strategy** Ask *Why do you suppose Hannah is crying?* (because her parakeet has flown away) Remind children that one action can cause another. Ask *What is the result?* (Hannah cries.)

- **Phonics Skill** Have children find the words *won't, didn't,* and *don't* in the text. Show on the board how these contractions are formed from *will not, did not,* and *do not.*

Turn to page 8 – Book Talk

"Joe won't be frightened of cats," Hannah told her dad, "or know how to get food."

Hannah left food and water on the balcony in case Joe came looking there.

Although she had telephoned friends and asked them to look out for Joe, no one called.

Sometimes at night, Hannah lay in bed and cried.

Revisiting the Text

After five days had gone by, Hannah didn't cry any more, but she was still sad.

"I'll buy you another bird," her dad told her.

"I don't want another bird," Hannah replied. "I want Joe."

But now Hannah was afraid she would never see Joe again.

Future Vocabulary

- Ask *What is Hannah doing?* (crying in bed) Explain the difference between crying just a little and sobbing. Ask them to use the word *sob* in a sentence.

- Explain that *sob* can also mean "to speak using a tearful voice." For page 7, the author could have written *"I don't want another bird," Hannah sobbed.*

Now revisit pages 8–9

During Reading

Book Talk

- Ask *What do you think is happening in this illustration?* (Hannah sees a bird that could be Joe.) *This bird is yellow and gray. Could this parakeet be Joe? Why would he be gray?* (He is dirty or muddy.)

- **Phonics Skill** Write the words *must not* on the board, then have children locate the word *mustn't* in the text. Ask for a volunteer to show how to make the contraction *mustn't* from *must not*.

- Have children find the word *parakeet* in the text. Explain that parakeets can be different colors and that some can be taught to speak.

Turn to page 10 – Book Talk

Chapter 2

A Bump Under the Jacket

Hannah and her mom went to the park on Saturday.

Near the swings, Hannah saw a sudden flash of yellow. It was a bird, and watching it land made Hannah think of Joe. Joe was yellow all over, not yellow and gray like this bird.

Revisiting the Text

Then she saw that the gray part was mud. The bird *was* yellow all over. When it turned its head, Hannah saw it was a parakeet with little black eyes.

Joe! It was Joe!

What should she do now? She mustn't frighten him.

Future Vocabulary
- Ask *How can Hannah recognize Joe even though he's all muddy?* (because he's her bird and she knows him well)
- Explain that *recognize* can also mean "to acknowledge achievements by giving awards," and use the word in a sentence.

Now revisit pages 10–11

During Reading

Book Talk

- Ask *What has Hannah done in this illustration?* (thrown her jacket over Joe) *Where is Joe?* (under the jacket)

- **Fluency Skill** Have children read page 10 aloud, varying the loudness and softness of their voice to reflect what's going on in the story.

- **Comprehension Strategy**
  Ask *Can Joe fly now?* (no) *Why can't he fly?* (Hannah threw the jacket over him.) *What is the first action that happened, or the cause?* (Hannah threw the jacket.) *What is the second event, or the result?* (Joe can't fly.)

Turn to page 12 – Book Talk

Hannah turned and grabbed the jacket from Mom, who made a surprised noise.

"Sssshhh," said Hannah.

She moved toward Joe and threw the jacket.

"Yes!" she cried.

There was a little bump underneath the jacket, and Hannah knew that the bump was Joe.

"Mom! Come and help me!" she called.

10

Revisiting the Text

Future Vocabulary

- Ask *In this illustration, is Hannah clutching anything?* (no) *What does it mean to clutch something?* (to hold something tightly)

- Say *A woman's purse can be called a clutch. Some cars have a pedal called a clutch.* Have volunteers say sentences using these definitions.

Now revisit pages 12–13

During Reading

Book Talk

- Ask *Where is Joe now?* (in the cage) *Do you think he is frightened?* (no) *Why do people keep parakeets in cages?* (to keep them safe)

- Have children locate the word *balcony* in the text. Ask *Do you think Joe is safer on the balcony or in his cage?* (in his cage)

- **Phonics Skill** Have children locate the words *let's, it's,* and *you've* in the text. Ask for volunteers to show on the board how these contractions are formed from *let us*, *it is*, and *you have*.

Turn to page 14 – Book Talk

Chapter 3

At Last!

Back in his cage, Joe ate and drank a lot. Later he sat on his perch cleaning his feathers. Hannah sat watching him. "I wonder where you've been?" she said.

The next day, Hannah hung Joe's cage on the balcony. Joe's clean feathers looked as yellow as the sun.

"It's a beautiful morning," said Mom. "Let's have breakfast outside."

12

Revisiting the Text

While Mom and Dad sat down near Joe's cage, Hannah brought out the orange juice. She felt very happy, so she joked with Mom and Dad. "Hello," she smiled, "I'm your waitress."

Someone else said something. "Hello, I'm Joe."

They all stared at Joe's cage.

Future Vocabulary
- Ask children to study the illustration on page 12. Ask *Do you recognize these two adults?* (yes) *Who are they?* (Hannah's parents)

Now revisit pages 14–15

During Reading

Book Talk

- **Fluency Skill** Have children read page 14 aloud, varying the loudness and softness of their voices to reflect what's going on in the story.

- **Comprehension Strategy** Ask *Why is the family smiling?* (Joe is safely back in his cage.) *So if Joe being in his cage is the cause, what is the effect of this event?* (The family smiles.)

- **Phonics Skill** Have children locate the words *I'm* and *he's* in the text. Ask for volunteers to show on the board how to make these contractions.

Turn to page 16 – Book Talk

"Hello, I'm Joe. Hello, I'm Joe," said Hannah's pet.

"Goodness me!" said Mom. "Joe's talking, at last!"

Hannah was excited. "Now I should teach him to say where he lives, just in case he's ever lost again."

Revisiting the Text

Dad grinned. "He would have to be very clever to say that!"

Future Vocabulary

- Say *Hannah has a pitcher of juice. Is she clutching the pitcher?* (No, she's just holding it.) *What would it look like if she were clutching the pitcher?* (She would be grasping it tightly.)

Go to page T5 – Revisiting the Text

During Reading

Book Talk
- Leave this page for children to discover on their own when they read the book individually.

Individual Reading
Have each child read the entire book at his or her own pace while remaining in the group.

Go to page T5 – Revisiting the Text

"Are you that clever?" Hannah asked her pet.

"Hello, I'm Joe," he replied.

Hannah shook her head. "I'd better teach you something easy."

"I think so," said Mom and Dad together.

 During independent work time, children can read the online book at:
www.rigbyflyingcolors.com

16

Revisiting the Text

Future Vocabulary
- Use the notes on the right-hand pages to develop oral vocabulary that goes beyond the text. These vocabulary words first appear in future texts. These words are: *clutch*, *recognize*, and *sob*.

Turn back to page 1

Reading Vocabulary Review
Activity Sheet: Word Map

- Introduce the word *frightened*.
- Together with children, complete the Word Map. Have children describe what people do when they are *frightened* and give examples of *frighten*ing things.

Comprehension Strategy Review
Use Interactive Modeling Card: Comparing Two Fiction Books

- Brainstorm with children another fiction book that reminds them of *Hello, I'm Joe.*
- Have children help you list the sequence of events of both books on the board. Complete the chart by filling in the columns.

Phonics Review
- Have children review the text for these contractions: *I'm, you'd, don't, won't, didn't, mustn't, you've, it's, let's, he's,* and *I'd.*
- Write these words in a column on the board. Next to each contraction, have volunteers write the two words used to form it.

Fluency Review
- Partner children and have them take turns reading page 10 in the text.
- Remind them that their voice should grow softer in quieter moments to create drama. Their voice should grow louder in the exciting parts.

Reading-Writing Connection
Activity Sheet: Character Profile

To assist children with linking reading and writing:
- Have children complete the Character Profile for Hannah.
- Using this information, have children write a want ad for Hannah to help her find what she wants.

4 Assessment

Assessing Future Vocabulary

Work with each child individually. Ask questions that elicit each child's understanding of the Future Vocabulary words. Note each child's responses:

- Which is easier to clutch—a pencil or a house?
- If you recognize a friend, what should you do?
- Why do people sob?

Assessing Comprehension Strategy

Work with each child individually. Note each child's understanding of cause and effect:

- What did Dad do on the balcony?
- When he left the door open, what happened?
- When Hannah saw Joe at the park, what did she do? How did this affect Joe?
- Which comes first, the cause or the effect?

Assessing Phonics

Work with each child individually. Turn to page 12 and have each child read this page aloud, pointing out the contractions either during or after the reading. Note each child's responses for understanding the identifying and reading of contractions:

- Did each child pronounce the contractions correctly?
- Did each child recognize which words are contractions?
- Point to the contractions and ask each child for the two words used to form each contraction.

Assessing Fluency

Have each child read page 10 to you. Note each child's understanding of varying the use of loudness and softness when reading phrases:

- Did each child use a softer voice when Hannah says "Sssshhh"?
- Did each child use a louder voice when Hannah calls for help from her mom?
- Did each child use a normal tone of voice with the rest of the text?

Interactive Modeling Cards

Meaning Map

clutch	She clutched the paper in her hand.
Word	Sentence

I think the word means: to hold something

The definition I found: to grasp or hold tightly

A new sentence that shows the meaning: I had to clutch the bowl so I wouldn't drop it.

Comparing Two Fiction Books

	Book Title *Hello, I'm Joe*	Book Title *Cupcakes*
Setting in Time and Place	present-day, large city	present-day, home
Main Character	Hannah	Eddie
Story Problem	Hannah's parakeet Joe is lost.	Eddie breaks his mom's favorite bowl.
How the Character Handles the Problem	She cries.	Eddie hides the broken bowl.
Solution	Hannah uses a jacket to catch Joe.	Eddie promises his mom he won't hide things.

Directions: With children, fill in the Meaning Map using the word *clutch*.

Directions: With children, fill in the Comparing Two Fiction Books chart for *Hello, I'm Joe* and another book the class has read.

Discussion Questions
- What words did Hannah try to teach Joe? (Literal)
- Which characters felt bad that Joe flew away? (Critical Thinking)
- What will Dad likely always do with the balcony door in the future? (Inferential)

T7

Activity Sheets

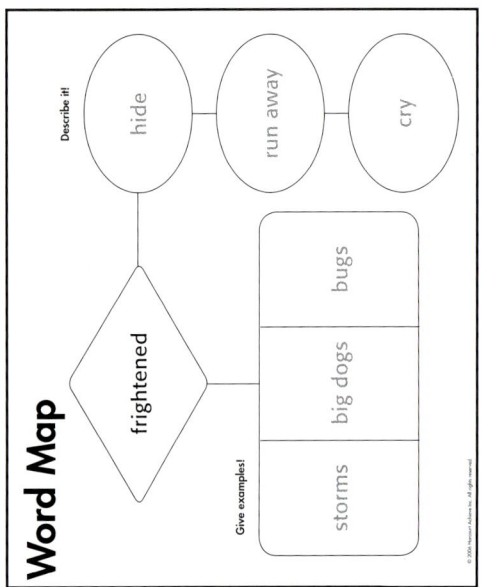

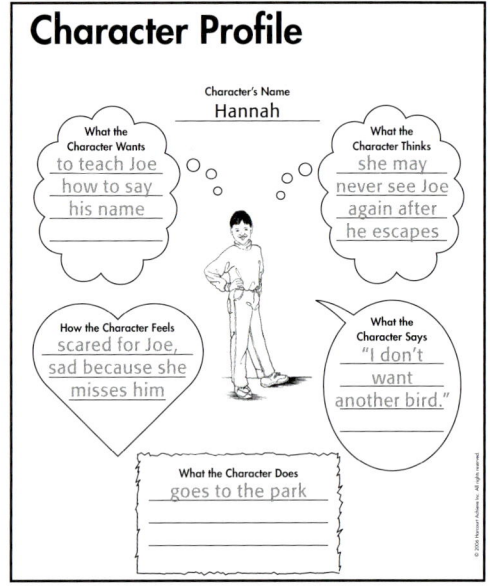

Directions: Have children fill in the Word Map using the word *frightened*.

Directions: Have children fill in the Character Profile for Hannah in *Hello, I'm Joe* and then write a want ad to help Hannah find what she wants.
Optional: Have children think of another story about Hannah and Joe and write a description of the problem in that story.